101 Questions About

Desert Life

by Alice Jablonsky

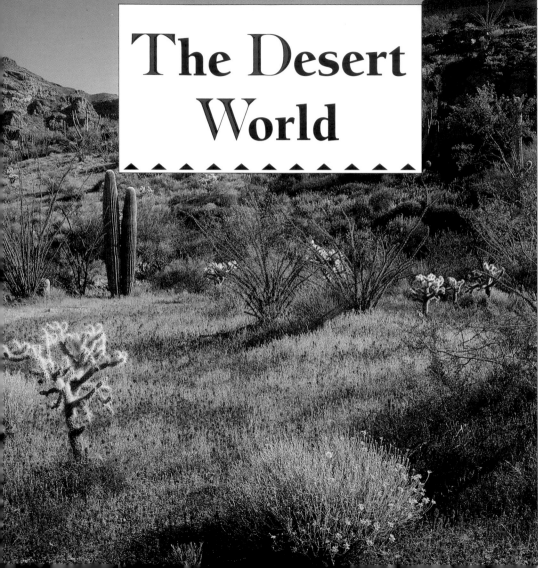

The Desert World

What is a desert?

A desert is an arid place that receives, on average, less than ten inches of rain, and occasionally snow, a year. The timing and total amount of rain vary dramatically during the year, and from year to year. When it does rain in the desert, it can literally pour. Rain typically falls in amounts greater than the soil can absorb, and flash flooding from runoff is common.

The scanty moisture a desert absorbs tends to evaporate rapidly, especially on hot, sunny days. With low relative humidity and little or no cloud cover, summer daytime temperatures soar above one hundred degrees while nights can be very chilly. Rapid heating and cooling leads to high winds, which increase evaporation.

Sonoran desert

Is there more than one desert in North America?

The Great North American Desert stretches from eastern Oregon south into northern Mexico. Within this vast region are four geographically distinct areas: the Great Basin, Mojave, Sonoran, and Chihuahuan deserts. Each desert has its own plant and animal community.

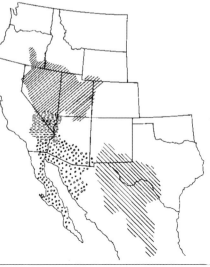

▨ *Great Basin*
▩ *Mojave*
▦ *Sonoran*
▧ *Chihuahuan*

Why are there deserts in the American Southwest?

All deserts are formed by a combination of geography, scanty rainfall, and extreme temperatures.

The Sonoran and Chihuahuan deserts of the American Southwest are located in a zone of latitude where high pressure, caused by descending dry air, is common.

The Mojave and Great Basin deserts lie in the rain shadow of the Sierra Nevada. This great mountain range acts as a barrier to moist air that comes from the Pacific Ocean, and much of the water vapor falls as rain or snow on the western side.

How can people survive in a desert?

Life in a desert can be challenging for people. Your body is not well adapted to cope with the abundance of sun and lack of water.

The average healthy person cannot survive for long in open desert without water, especially in the summer. As the temperature rises, your heart pumps more quickly, circulating blood faster through surface blood vessels. Sweat glands also release more moisture to cool your body through evaporation, yet the air is so dry you may not notice you are perspiring.

The risks of of heat stroke and dehydration are great. You must compensate by wearing sensible clothing, avoiding prolonged exposure, and drinking plenty of water.

Kit fox

How do animals survive in a desert?

The animal species that live in the desert are survivors of natural selection. Over time they have developed the physical characteristics and behaviors appropriate for this challenging environment. They are able to conserve water, and most avoid activity during the heat of the day. Some species even estivate, or sleep, through the hottest, driest months.

Pocket mouse

Why don't I see many desert animals during the daytime?

During the summer, there are some days that are so hot you'd rather stay inside your air conditioned house. Well, imagine hiking in a desert on a July afternoon, when the air temperature can soar above 120 degrees. Daytime temperatures are often too hot for many small animals. They burrow in the ground during the heat of day or find a nice shady spot under a cactus or shrub. At night, animals can hunt for food in cooler temperatures.

Do Southwest deserts have winter?

Yes. In fact, they have all four seasons: spring, summer, fall, and winter. Winter is an important season when many deserts get the moisture plants need to grow and bloom in the spring. The Great Basin Desert is even called a "cool" desert, because half of its moisture falls in the winter as snow. Some years snow can even dust the Sonoran Desert.

Where do desert animals go in winter?

All creatures are adapted for living through winter. Some birds migrate to warmer climates. Others, including roadrunners, quail, and kestrels, are able to live in the Southwest deserts year-round. Although the Great Basin and Mojave deserts have few trees or other large plants that can provide shelter, the desert earth offers a safe home to insects, reptiles, and mammals. Certain animals hibernate, or sleep through winter, in protected places. Others simply stay in warm burrows and rest there for days or weeks at a time until they get hungry.

When is the best season to see animals in a desert?

Desert animals are most active in late winter and early spring. Insects are most abundant then and are good sources of food for spiders, lizards, and birds. As in most environments, animals give birth in spring, when food is most plentiful.

Are there year-round rivers in the Southwest deserts?

Rivers that begin in distant, wetter, mountainous regions flow through some deserts. The Colorado River, for example, wends through the Great Basin, Mojave, and Sonoran deserts; the Gila River bisects the Sonoran Desert in Arizona, and the Rio Grande cuts through the Chihuahuan Desert. The Colorado River and other rivers that flow through the Southwest provide only part of the water that is used by people in the desert. In some states, including Arizona, most of the water that people use is pumped from deep underground.

Why will I sometimes find palm trees or other big green plants in the middle of a desert?

In deserts, underground water sometimes rises to the surface, forming springs or seeps. A fertile green area called an *oasis* may exist near such a water source. Lush vegetation, including grasses and trees, grows near these water sources. An oasis provides people and animals with water, food, and shelter.

What is quicksand?

Quicksand occurs when water flowing through sand mixes with it to form a thick fluid. The quicksand may look solid and firm, but if you stepped on the rippling part of the sand it would wiggle like gelatin. If you stood on it, you might start to sink, because the grains are too far apart to support the weight of a person or large animal.

How could I escape from quicksand?

If you were caught in quicksand, you could free yourself by stretching out on the surface, as if you were floating on your back in the water. Then you could slowly roll to firmer ground. Or you could try bending one knee, shifting your weight forward, and then slowly dragging the other leg out of the mucky sand. To escape quicksand you must think quickly and move with purpose. A person who panics and thrashes about may only sink deeper. That's what usually happens to animals that get stuck.

What are fossils?

Fossils are the mineralized remains of ancient animals or plants. They range in size from huge dinosaur bones to tiny plants and animals, which can only be seen under a microscope. Deserts are good places to see fossils because wind and erosion expose the lower layers of rock.

How do fossils form?

It takes millions of years and very special conditions for a fossil to form. After the soft tissue decays, minerals slowly seep into the hard parts, including shells, bones, teeth, or wood. As these minerals build up, the remains become heavier and stronger and keep their original shapes. Ultimately, the organic matter is completely replaced by minerals.

Creosote bush

How do plants survive in the desert?

Desert plants have become adapted in different ways to obtain and save water. Cactuses have shallow, wide-spreading root systems. They soak up water quickly after a storm. Leaves of the creosote bush are coated with a thick wax that keeps water from evaporating. Other desert plants have very deep roots. The roots of a mesquite tree, for example, can reach water more than one hundred feet underground.

Many desert plants are annuals, which means that they live only one season. Their seeds may lie dormant in the ground for years during long dry spells. Given the right amount of water at the right time, the seeds sprout very quickly. Plants grow, bloom, produce new seeds, and die, often in a short span of time. A soaking fall rain can transform a desert into a spring wonderland of flowers.

Why do cactus plants have sharp spines?

People once thought that cactus plants had spines for protection against plant-eating animals, but it is more likely that spines evolved from leaves as a water-conserving adaptation, to minimize transpiration.

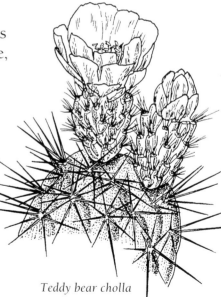

Teddy bear cholla

How can animals eat a prickly cactus and not hurt themselves?

Jackrabbits, ground squirrels, pack rats, peccaries, and several other animals are not discouraged by cactus spines. In fact, pig-like peccaries often eat the cactus and the spines. They have developed tough, leathery skin around their mouths that helps them tear off the juicy fruit, and their digestive systems have adapted to pass sharp objects through. The antelope ground squirrel climbs on top of barrel cactus spines to eat the fruit at the center. Others animals carefully avoid the spines or bite them off to nibble on the fleshy cactus. Birds gingerly build nests among prickly branches of cholla (CHOY-yah) cactus.

Can people eat desert plants?

Desert-dwelling peoples have depended upon plants for food as well as for other needs. Long ago, people crafted mesquite tree limbs into bows and arrows or used them as fuel, and the beans were a source of food. Today, you may even use mesquite wood chips on the barbecue. The waxy creosote bush has provided medicine for colds, stomach cramps, and infected wounds. Fruits of some plants, like cactuses and the fan palm, are still harvested and eaten. Ever try prickly pear jelly? It's very sweet and tasty. The Tohono O'odham people in Arizona have a festival after the saguaro fruit is harvested.

What other uses have people found for desert plants?

Fan palm fronds were once used for building shelters and making baskets and sandals. Today beautiful baskets are woven from them.

Other plants also have been useful in making clothing. The long fibers of agave and yucca plants were once used to weave sandals, clothing, decorations, and nets and pouches used to catch animals.

Desert fan palm

(21) What is that tall cactus with arms?

The saguaro (suh-WAH-row) is the tallest cactus that grows in the Sonoran Desert of Southern Arizona.

The saguaro expands like an accordion, which enables it to store water in its long trunk and arms. A large saguaro is a living storage tower that can hold hundreds of gallons of water. Some saguaros may live for as long as two hundred years and grow as tall as fifty feet.

They are favorite perching and nesting places for Gila (HEE-lah) woodpeckers, gilded flickers, pygmy and elf owls, red-tailed hawks, and many other birds.

(22) Why are there holes in a saguaro trunk?

Each spring Gila woodpeckers and gilded flickers chip nest holes in saguaro trunks. They raise their young inside these cavities. Since woodpeckers make a new nest hole each year, their old homes are available to new tenants. The nest holes are also safe from predators, which cannot climb up the steep, spiny saguaro trunks.

Gila woodpecker

(23) Do these holes hurt the saguaro?

After a bird pecks its nest in the fleshy stem, the saguaro cactus heals quickly by forming a scab-like shell around the injured tissue. This prevents infection and the loss of precious water.

(24) How many kinds of animals live in a saguaro?

More than a dozen species of birds nest in saguaro holes. Since nest holes make such good homes, small mammals, including bats, pack rats, and cactus mice, often move in. Lizards, insects, and spiders also seek refuge inside saguaros. Other bird species, including the greater road-runner, cactus wren, white-winged dove, and mourning dove, build nests outside in the crooks of saguaro arms.

How do animals find water in the desert?

Every living thing needs water to stay alive, from mammals, including coyotes, cottontails, and mice, to even the smallest butterfly or beetle.

Areas with permanent standing or flowing water are rare, yet in many places, particularly seemingly dry washes and arroyos, water may be found only a few feet underground. Coyotes may dig down for a drink. These "coyote wells" attract birds, mice, and other animals. Animals like the tiny kangaroo rat only get water from the food they eat.

Others lap dew from plants in the morning. Bristly peccaries roaming the Sonoran and Chihuahuan deserts cannot get all the moisture they need from plants, although they eat prickly pear cactus. Peccaries, which look and sound like their distant wild-pig relatives, must also drink water from streams or ponds. You might notice their small hoof prints marking trails that lead to water.

Why is it so hard to *see* desert animals?

Nearly all of the desert landscape is light-colored, and so are nearly all desert animals. During the summer, we tend to wear lighter colors to stay cool. Light colors reflect sunlight, while dark colors absorb it. The lighter shades of desert animals help them avoid overheating. Light colors also give some animals protection from predators. A sandy-colored rodent or lizard is much harder to see against a sandy-colored background.

Can desert animals get sunburned?

Unlike people, desert creatures have fur, scales, or other body coverings that prevent their skin from getting sunburned.

How do desert animals beat the heat?

Desert animals must find a way to escape the sun's rays; otherwise, their body temperatures would rise rapidly and most would die. Some animals, including amphibians, reptiles, and small mammals, burrow underground. Others pant, which cools the body by evaporating water from the tongue.

How can I find animals in the desert?

The best way to find animals in the desert is to learn where they are most likely to be found and when they are most active. Look for burrows and nests in more heavily vegetated areas, especially along washes. Animals are most apt to be out when the sun is not.

Insects, Spiders and Scorpions

Tarantula hawk

How can insects live in the desert?

Desert plants attract many animals, including those insects that get nectar from their flowers, birds that nest in their branches, and rodents that eat seeds and leaves.

Insect bodies have a special feature that helps them survive in deserts. Most adults have a thin, waxy covering just below the surface that prevents water loss into the air.

Insects can meet their small water needs from their food or from dew or absorb water from the air or soil. All insects protect themselves from water loss by avoiding the sun at its hottest.

dung beetle

Are there cockroaches even in the desert?

Yes. The desert cockroach lives underground in sandy soil. To avoid the heat of day, it moves down a foot or more into the earth. There the soil is cool and holds some moisture. The cockroach can absorb water through its body from the damp sand.

What is a dung beetle?

A dung beetle collects the droppings of mammals, shapes them into balls, and buries them in the ground. It uses this animal waste as food. Often they collect more than they actually eat. The waste breaks down more quickly underground than it would lying on the dry earth. The buried droppings soon add nutrients to the soil.

Will I see butterflies in the desert?

Delicate, colorful butterflies can be seen in all four desert regions, and are common after a good rainfall. There are many species, and each gathers pollen and nectar from a particular kind of desert wildflower or flowering shrub. The monarch, perhaps the most easily recognized species and the only butterfly that migrates north and south like birds, visits the deserts of the Southwest during its journey.

Desert swallowtail butterfly

What makes the yucca moth so special?

The yucca and the yucca moth need each other to reproduce.

In the spring, a yucca moth will pollinate a yucca flower and lay her eggs there. As the flower develops into a fruit, the eggs hatch and the larvae feed on the seeds of the flower. In the fall, the larvae drop to the ground and bury themselves a few inches deep. There they spin cocoons over the winter months. Next spring, the adult moths will emerge from their cocoons to begin the cycle over again.

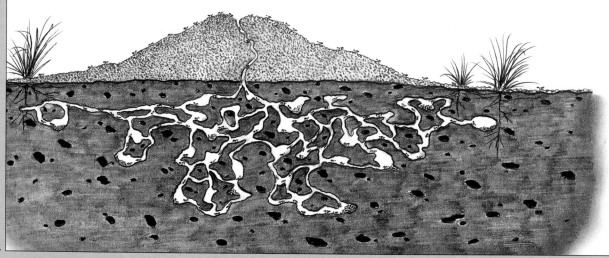

35
What kind of ants make those huge anthills?

Harvester ants are very good at digging holes and piling large mounds of desert soil around the opening to their home. These ants live on the seeds of wildflowers, grasses, and other plants. The colony digs a complicated tunnel system in the ground — sometimes ten to fifteen feet deep.

On warm summer days, the ants come up to search for food. Be careful: They can give you a painful bite.

36
Why do harvester ants make such big tunnels?

In their deep tunnels harvester ants are insulated from both cold and heat. They bring seeds into the tunnels and store them in grain rooms. The seed supply provides food during the seasons when the desert offers little to eat. Other chambers are dug to shelter eggs and developing larvae.

37
Do all ants like to eat seeds?

No. Some species will eat almost anything, including bits of food you leave on the table or even other ants. Honey ants store a sugary liquid they collect from food they eat. Young worker ants collect the juice until their bodies swell up like balloons. In the months to come, they become living storage containers and give off food droplets for the rest of the colony.

38
What kind of animal is an ant lion?

An ant lion is the developing young, or *larva*, of a lacewing insect. The ant lion digs a cone-shaped pit in loose, sandy soil and waits near the bottom. When an insect stumbles into the pit, the ant lion snaps it up.

Where would I most likely find a scorpion?

Scorpions seek shelter from the heat in crevices or under rocks during the day. They come out at night to hunt for insects and other prey.

How do scorpions have babies?

The scorpion's young are born alive. They are light-colored at birth and their bodies contain a yolk that nourishes them until they are old enough to hunt their own food. Until then, they ride on their mother's back.

Do all scorpions sting?

There are more than twenty species of scorpions in the desert Southwest. Although all of them are known to have stingers, not all are deadly. Both male and female scorpions sting and may do so in self-defense as well as to catch food.

How does a scorpion sting?

Although people are afraid of being stung by a scorpion, the venom of most species is no more dangerous to humans than a wasp's.

A scorpion captures and holds its prey with heavy pincers on its front legs. It stings by injecting venom into the prey from a gland in its tail. The venom affects the nervous system and the prey becomes paralyzed. Eventually, the venom destroys the surrounding tissues.

What is the largest desert spider?

The largest spider in the desert is the fuzzy tarantula. In the Sonoran Desert it may grow to have a six-inch legspan. That is about as wide as the distance between your thumb and little finger if you spread your fingers apart.

In spite of their size, these spiders are gentle creatures that only bite if threatened. In the fall, male tarantulas may be seen during the day, looking for females and food. Female tarantulas are rarely seen outside their burrows.

Can a bite from a tarantula hurt me?

These spiders use venom to kill their insect prey. Although its bite may be painful, no tarantula found in the United States is dangerous to people.

(45)

Do tarantulas spin webs?

Tarantulas live in web-lined holes in the ground. About twenty species of tarantulas are found throughout the Southwest.

Like other tarantulas, the desert tarantula spends most of its time in a burrow. When cold weather comes, it plugs up the opening and waits for the return of warm weather.

(46)

How long can a tarantula live?

Female tarantulas may live for a long time — some have survived for thirty years.

(47)

What kind of a bird is a tarantula hawk?

Tarantula hawks are not birds; they are large wasps that hunt tarantulas to feed their young.

When a female wasp is ready to lay an egg, she finds a tarantula and stings it. This paralyzes the spider. The wasp drags the spider to a hole in the ground, lays her egg on the spider, and buries it. When the wasp larva hatches, it will feed on the spider. The wasp must catch a spider for every egg she lays.

Reptiles, Amphibians and Fish

Desert pupfish

(48)

Are there fish that can live in the desert?

Fish need a continuing supply of water. Although it is not common in the desert, there is still enough water to support more than twenty species of desert fish in the Southwest.

Look for them in small streams and springs in the desert regions of Arizona, California, Nevada, and New Mexico. The tiny desert pupfish, often less than an inch long, can survive in water temperatures of more than one hundred degrees.

Tiger salamander

How can water creatures live in places where there isn't permanent water?

For most water animals in the desert, a brief shower is all they need to survive. A good example is the desert shrimp. It lives only in the brief summer rainy season when rain pools form. The eggs of desert shrimp remain dormant during dry periods. When a puddle forms, the shrimp hatch, mate, and lay new eggs, all within a few weeks.

What happens when the rain pool dries up?

When the pool dries up, the adults die. Many of their eggs will survive in the dry soil and hatch when a pool forms again.

How can toads and frogs live in the desert?

Amphibians, like toads, frogs, and salamanders, die if they dry out, so they must seek shelter in basins where water collects. Amphibians spend most of their lives deep underground. They come out only during the brief rainy period. After a very short breeding time of weeks or even days, they return underground until the following year. Desert toads have been very successful in surviving the hot, dry climate of the desert.

What makes desert toads so special?

When drought sets in, the Couch's spadefoot toad keeps moist by borrowing into damp ground. The spadefoot retains moisture with a covering of dry, partially shed skin, then goes into a deep summer sleep. The toad's nap can last for months. The toad remains underground until desert conditions are just right. When a storm breaks, the toad wakes up, digs out, and heads for the nearest puddle to find a mate, lay and fertilize eggs, and soak up moisture.

Is a horned toad really a toad?

A horned "toad," despite its rounded shape, is not an amphibian. It is really a horned lizard, a reptile. Horned lizards flatten their bodies as much as possible, and turn perpendicular to the sun's rays to warm themselves, and parallel to cool down.

Horned lizard

How do snakes and lizards live in the desert?

Reptiles, including snakes, lizards, and tortoises, have no means of controlling body temperature, so they must avoid too much heat.

Throughout the day lizards go in and out of the shade to keep from becoming too hot or too cold. Snakes and lizards get enough water for their needs from the food they eat. Scales on their skin help resist drying.

Common kingsnake

How do reptiles have babies?

Most reptiles lay their eggs in the soil, where there is usually enough dampness for them to hatch. Others, including rattlesnakes and some spiny lizards, give birth to live young. Either way, the the young are born looking like tiny adults. Reptile young do not have to go through a tadpole phase in water like amphibians, such as frogs and toads.

Are there more snakes or more lizards in the desert?

If you take a walk in the deserts of the Southwest, you will probably see more lizards than any other animal. Compared to the number of lizards, there are not a great many snakes in the desert.

Most lizards are active in the daytime. If you are quiet and watchful, you can see them scurrying around. Desert snakes hunt mostly at night, when it is cooler.

What is a chuckwalla?

A chuckwalla is a large lizard with a big belly. It has loose folds of skin around its neck and shoulders. It can be found primarily in the Sonoran and Great Basin deserts, basking in the morning sunlight to warm up its body temperature.

Chuckwalla

Where is a chuckwalla's favorite hiding place?

When danger threatens, the chuckwalla often retreats to a deep, narrow crevice. It crawls into it until firmly wedged between the walls. Then it gulps air and pumps itself up so it can't be pulled out by a predator.

What is the largest lizard in the United States?

The Gila (HEE-lah) monster, found in the Sonoran and Mojave deserts, ranges in length from eighteen to twenty-four inches.

Are any lizards in the desert venomous?

The only venomous lizard in the United States is the Gila monster. It's venomous bite can overcome small animals such as rodents and baby birds. It also eats the eggs of ground-nesting birds. The lizard's flickering tongue reports on temperature changes and helps the animal find prey.

Why does the Gila monster have such a big, fat tail?

When there is a lot of food around, the Gila monster eats as much as possible. Food it digests beyond its daily needs is stored in its tail in the form of fat. This lizard lives on this fat when no other food is available.

Gila monster

19

Why does the fringe-toed lizard have fringed toes?

The fringe-toed lizard lives only in sandy areas in the Sonoran and Mojave deserts. The fringes are scales on its long hind toes that make it easier to run on sand. They also help the lizard push its body underground. The toes open outward to help the lizard push loose sand away from its body.

This lizard can dash over hot sand up to fifteen miles per hour. To escape the sun or danger, it dives into the sand and "swims" beneath the surface by wiggling its body. It can remain buried for a long time, breathing air trapped in the spaces between grains of sand.

(63)

Do snakes have ears?

Snakes do not have ears and must depend on their eyes and tongue to hunt. They also are very sensitive to vibrations on the ground, which can alert them to approaching danger or a possible meal.

(64)

Why does a snake stick out its tongue?

A snake's forked tongue helps it track down prey. As the snake hunts for a meal, it is constantly flicking out its tongue. Each time the tongue returns to the snake's mouth it brings clues from the snake's surroundings to a hollow in the roof of the mouth. The hollow is lined with sensitive cells, which enable the snake to "taste" the track of its prey.

The forked tongue provides more surface area and thus greater sensitivity, so the snake can find its prey more easily.

How and why do rattlesnakes rattle?

A rattlesnake's tail has separate segments of horny material formed by scales that are left behind when the snake molts, or sheds its skin. Each time the snake molts, a new segment is formed.

When a rattlesnake feels threatened, its powerful muscles vibrate its tail very quickly. This causes the horny segments to rub against one another. The sound of the rattle alerts animals to stay away.

How many kinds of rattlesnakes are found in Southwest deserts?

There are about a dozen species of rattlers in Southwest deserts. The western diamondback is the largest snake in the western United States, and can grow up to seven feet in length.

All snakes hibernate, and many estivate as well. In the southern deserts rattlesnakes may awaken and move about for a few hours during winter warm spells.

How do rattlesnakes find their prey in the dark?

Rattlesnakes, sidewinders, and other members of the pit viper family have a special way of finding prey.

Two small pits in front of their eyes are sensitive heat detectors. These pits are capable of sensing rises in temperature caused by the presence of a warm-blooded animal.

The heat detectors inform the snake where and how far away the prey is. This helps the snake make an accurate strike in total darkness.

The tongue helps, too.

Western diamondback rattlesnake

21

What is the most venomous snake in the desert?

The Arizona coral snake has the strongest venom. This shy snake is rarely seen by people and spends most of the hot day under rocks. At night, it slithers out to hunt for food.

Wide red, black, and yellow bands along its body make it easy to recognize. But you may be fooled by the non-poisonous Sonoran shovelnose, which looks almost like the coral snake. Experts can tell the difference by the pattern of the colored bands on the bodies of the two snakes. The "copycat" shovelnose has protection from snake-eating birds and other animals, which are fooled by the brightly colored bands and stay away.

The Mojave rattlesnake also has potent venom, and is larger and more commonly encountered than the coral snake.

How do snakes move without legs?

Most snakes move by undulating their ribs, causing waves of movement to pass from head to tail. The characteristic "S" curve occurs as the snake alternately tightens muscles on one side of the body as it relaxes those on the opposite side. The combination of these forward and lateral movements, transfered to the belly scales, moves the snake forward.

The sidewinder rattlesnake uses a distinctive sideways motion to cross the sand. The sidewinder touches the ground at two points and thrusts the rest of its body sideways. The sideways motion leaves rows of parallel tracks.

sidewinder rattlesnake

What is the difference between a desert tortoise and a turtle?

A tortoise lives on dry land, while a turtle spends most of its time in water.

Why does the desert tortoise move so slowly?

The desert tortoise has no need to move quickly because it carries its armor with it. At the first hint of danger it withdraws its head and limbs into its shell until it is safe for it to emerge. The slow lifestyle of the tortoise also allows it to conserve energy.

Doesn't the desert tortoise get hot carrying its big shell?

The thick shell actually helps the tortoise. Its hard shell provides shade and insulation, and leathery skin helps keep the water in its body from evaporating.

The desert tortoise also can escape the heat by burrowing underground.

How does a desert tortoise drink water?

These reptiles are able to change some of their food into water. They also can drink water directly by submerging their heads, sometimes for amazingly long periods. They store water in sacs under their shells. A full supply — about a pint — can last through an entire dry season.

Desert Birds

Red-tailed hawk

Do feathers make a bird feel hot?

Feathers actually keep heat and ultraviolet rays away from the bird's skin in summer and keep the cold out in winter.

Some birds cool themselves by flapping the loose skin that hangs under their throats. Others pant by breathing with open mouths, the way coyotes do.

75

How do birds replace the moisture they lose?

Panting causes a loss of water, which birds must replace. They may get water from the plants or animals they eat. Seed eaters must have real drinking water and may fly miles every day to get a drink.

What are those big birds I sometimes see circling over one spot in the desert?

Turkey vultures are continually on the lookout for a dead creature on the desert floor. They have a keen sense of smell that alerts them to the presence of a dead animal.

Sometimes these scavengers will circle over a weakening animal, watching until it stops moving. Their excellent eyesight enables them to spot other hovering vultures at great distances — a sign that there's a meal nearby.

What is the smallest bird in the desert Southwest?

The smallest desert bird is the three-inch calliope hummingbird of the Sonoran Desert. It flits from plant to plant feeding on insects and nectar from flowers.

The elf owl — only about five inches tall — is the smallest owl in the desert. It makes its home in abandoned woodpecker holes in saguaro cactuses. The elf owl eats moths and other insects, and scorpions.

Calliope hummingbird

Elf owl

How did the cactus wren get its name?

The cactus wren builds its home in the protection of the spiny cholla cactus or in the crook of a saguaro arm. The wren's football-sized nest is made of grass stems and lined with feathers.

Wrens are able to fly in and around their nests and perch on cactus without being impaled because the have bony feet and a thick coat of feathers.

Cactus wren

Where else can a bird live in the desert?

Burrowing owls live in underground tunnels originally dug by another animal. Unlike other owls, they are often out in daylight, standing near the burrow entrance. In the evening and through the night they hunt insects and rodents.

Which birds build the largest nest in the desert?

Hawks and eagles build the largest nests.

Can a roadrunner fly?

Yes, a roadrunner can fly, but it is fast and nimble on the ground. It has wide claws and strong legs that help it run over the desert at speeds up to fifteen miles an hour. By flicking its foot-long tail to one side, it can turn in mid-stride. The tail, when spread and raised above the bird's back, brakes the roadrunner to a quick stop.

(82)

What does a roadrunner eat?

The roadrunner primarily eats insects, gophers, mice, bird eggs, and lizards. The greater roadrunner also has been known to catch and eat snakes. It grabs the snake with its sharp-clawed feet and pecks at the snake with its beak. Once it kills its prey, the bird starts to swallow it. Often the snake is too long for the bird to get down all at once. It may walk around for days ingesting an inch or two at a time.

(83)

Do all birds of prey use their feet to catch food?

Birds of prey, including hawks, eagles, and owls, have keen eyesight to spot an animal on the desert floor. They swoop down and snatch animals using their strong talons, and then take the meal back to their nest to eat.

The shrike, a bird with a strong hooked bill, eats large insects, such as grasshoppers. In the winter, when insects are hard to find, it will hunt lizards, small mice, or even other birds. Unlike other birds of prey, the shrike does not have strong talons for holding its prey. Instead, the shrike stabs the animal with its hooked beak. Then the bird hangs its dead prey on a thorn, cactus spine, or even barbed wire. With the animal thus pinned in place, the shrike can tear the flesh apart and eat it more easily.

Desert Mammals

Coyote

Kangaroo rat

Do all desert animals have to drink water?

Among animals of the desert Southwest, the tiny kangaroo rat is one of the few that never needs to drink water. It gets its moisture from the plants, insects, and dry seeds it eats. When a kangaroo rat finds food, it may stuff some of it into its fur-lined cheek pouches. Then it carries the food to its burrow for storage.

Like other animals, it produces water as it digests its food. All mammals produce this water, but only the kangaroo rat can survive on the tiny amount it produces because it uses it very efficiently.

How far can a kangaroo rat jump?

The kangaroo rat moves like a tiny version of its namesake, jumping as far as ten feet in a single bound. Large hind feet keep it from sinking into the sand, and its long, tufted tail helps it keep its balance and steer. By swinging its rudder-like tail to one side, it can change course quickly. This helps it escape predators like coyotes, foxes, owls, and snakes.

86

How did the pack rat get its name?

A woodrat, commonly known as a pack rat, collects all kinds of objects for its nest. These include sticks, cactus pieces, dung, bones, and any other objects it can readily carry. So, hold on to your small toys and keys when you go camping in the desert.

Jackrabbit

87

How is a jackrabbit different from a "regular" rabbit?

A jackrabbit is really a hare.

A hare is usually larger than a rabbit, and it has longer hind legs. The ears of a hare are also longer than those of a rabbit and are often tipped with black. Rabbits are born without fur and blind; jackrabbits are born furry and with their eyes open.

88

Why does a jackrabbit have such big ears?

Long ears help the jackrabbit hear if danger is near, but their primary function is to help the animal keep cool. They provide a large surface area for radiating body heat. This acts as a cooling system for the warm blood that is circulated through the thin tissue of the ears.

Do other animals have big ears?

In general, among families of animals that range widely, species that live in desert environments have larger ears than related species that inhabit colder areas.

The ears of these desert animals, like those of the jackrabbit, have evolved to help keep the animals cool. Other desert animals with heat-radiating ears include the mule deer and kit fox.

Kit fox

Why isn't the kit fox red?

The sandy-colored kit fox blends into the desert landscape. It is the size of a small house cat when grown.

The kit fox hunts rabbits, lizards, insects, and rodents — especially kangaroo rats. Hairs on the undersides of its feet enable the kit fox to run swiftly over soft sand and loose desert soil.

Why do coyotes howl at night?

By sending calls across the landscape, coyotes let other coyotes know their whereabouts.

When they communicate, coyotes use different sounds to mean different things. They woof softly to warn their young. A bark tells enemies to keep away. In the evening, several coyotes may "sing" in chorus. One starts with a string of sharp yips. Then it gives a growl. Other coyotes join in. Soon their song echoes across the desert.

What does a coyote eat?

The coyote is omnivorous, which means it will eat almost anything. Known to eat grasses, nuts, and cactus fruit, the coyote prefers to hunt mice, rabbits, insects, snakes, and lizards.

As it hunts, the coyote uses it sharp eyesight, keen hearing, and sensitive nose. It trots long distances in search of prey. Occasionally, a coyote will kill lambs and calves. Some people have tried to get rid of coyotes with guns, poisons, and traps.

Mountain lion

94

Does a bobcat look like a cat?

Sort of. A bobcat is about twice as large as an ordinary house cat. A bobcat's soft, tan fur is spotted with black. Fringes of long whiskers grow out from beneath its tufted ears. The bobcat's tail — with its black tip and white under-side — is only about six inches long. In fact, the cat is named for its stubby tail, which seems to be cut, or bobbed. The bobcat is the most common member of the cat family found in Southwest deserts. It stays well-hidden among rocks or in bushy thickets.

93

Is a mountain lion the same as a bobcat?

No. The mountain lion is known by several common names — cougar, catamount, and puma — but a bobcat is a different animal.

Mountain lions live in remote areas with deep canyons and steep cliffs. They prey mainly on deer, elk, hares, large game birds, and even bighorn sheep. The mountain lion grows to about six or seven feet in length. Its long, graceful tail helps the animal keep its balance while stalking, running, leaping, and climbing.

95

What does a bobcat like to eat?

Although relatively small, a bobcat can kill an animal several times its size. Perhaps that is why is it also known as a wildcat. Usually a bobcat goes after smaller prey. It hunts rabbits, hares, mice, and squirrels. Crouching low to the ground, it slowly creeps toward its prey, then swiftly pounces. It may leap as far as ten feet to catch its meal.

Bobcat

96

Is a ringtail a member of the cat family?

The slender, whiskered ringtail is not a cat at all. The dark rings on its bushy tail mark it as a member of the raccoon family.

97

When does the ringtail hunt?

Active at night, the ringtail roams desert forests and canyons throughout the Southwest. It feeds on small animals, fruits, and plants. It is a skilled climber and easily darts up and down trees. Its hind feet turn backward, and the animal can grasp the bark with its sharp claws when it dives into a trunk headfirst. Ringtails often sleep in small caves or between rocks.

bighorn sheep

How do bighorn sheep keep from falling down mountains?

Bighorn sheep are at home in rocky terrain. They can move quickly and easily on uneven ground. Each hoof has two toes. Rough pads on the bottom grip the surface of the ground. For an even better hold on slick slopes, a desert bighorn's toes can spread wide, enabling the animal to leap from rock to rock.

How big do the horns of bighorns get?

All wild rams and most ewes have horns. Unlike a deer's antlers, which drop off each winter, a sheep's horns grow longer every year. Most of the growth takes place in spring and summer, when the sheep can find plenty to eat. A bighorn ram's horns may weigh thirty pounds — perhaps more than all the bones in his body combined.

Which is the rarest animal in the desert Southwest?

Bighorn sheep were once plentiful in the Southwest, but their numbers have been reduced by hunting and the abundance of feral horse and burros, which graze on the same foods as bighorns and foul waterholes. Today only scattered bands of bighorns live in the four desert regions, but several state and national parks are reintroducing bighorns into areas where they once roamed in great numbers.

Bighorns usually live in remote, mountainous places. In the spring, many female bighorns, called ewes, pick their way along rock cliffs to give birth on high ledges, which are less accessible to predators.

Can I bring home things I find in the desert?

While visiting the desert, it is important to respect the plants, animals, and rock formations you find.

All living and non-living parts of the ecosystem are linked together in may ways. It is important to avoid disturbing a naturally functioning ecosystem. Some plants that are picked in seconds may have taken many years to grow. Animals taken as pets often cannot survive in captivity.

It is illegal to take home souvenirs from the desert. Leave the desert as you find it so its plants and animals can live in harmony and be there for others to enjoy.